MW00618095

Celebrating Babies

Created by
Tracy Porter

**Andrews McMeel
Publishing**
Kansas City

Celebrating Babies

A Treasury for New Mothers

*I love little children,
and it is not a slight thing*

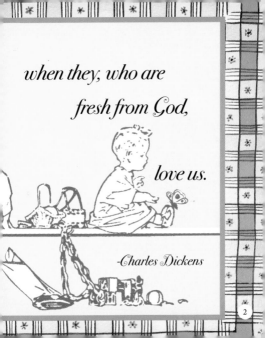

when they, who are

fresh from God,

love us.

-Charles Dickens

Dance, little baby,
dance up high!
Never mind, Baby,
mother is by.
Up to the ceiling,
down to the
ground,
Backwards
and forwards,
round and round!

4

When the first baby laughed
for the ✦ first time,
the laugh broke into
a thousand pieces
and they all went
skipping about,
and that was the
beginning of
fairies.

—J.M. Barrie, Peter Pan

Baby, little Babykins,
  Your eyes are like the sky

I love you, little Babykins,
  Excepting when you cry.

Baby, little Babykins,
  Your hair is silken floss

I love you, little Babykins
  Excepting when you're cross.

Baby, little Babykins,
  I love you anyway—

But when you smile
I love you more
  Than any other way.

8

We never know
the love of
our parents for us
till we have
become parents.

–Henry Ward Beecher

10

Smiling girls, rosy boys,

Come and buy my little toys,

Monkeys made of gingerbread,

And sugar horses painted red.

12

In the heavens above, the angels whispering to one another can find, among their burning terms of love, none so devotional as that of "Mother."

—Edgar Allen Poe

*Every babe born
into this world
is finer than
the last.*

Charles Dickens

Boys and girls
come out to play,
The moon does shine
as bright as day,
Leave your supper,
and leave your sleep,
And meet your playfellows
in the street;
Come with a whoop,
and come with a call
And come with a good will,
or not at all.

A mother understands what a child does not say.

—*Yiddish Proverb*

This little pig
went to market;

This little pig
stayed home;

This little pig
had roast beef;

This little pig had none;

And this little pig cried,

Wee, wee, wee!

All the way home.

Is not a young mother one of the sweetest sights life shows us?

William Makepeace Thackery

Where children are, there is the golden age.

—*Novalis*

Who ran to help me
when I fell,
and would some
pretty story tell,
Or kiss the place to
make it well?
My mother.

—Ann Taylor

Good night, dear children

Soft your nest

And fair the dreams that

Charm your rest.

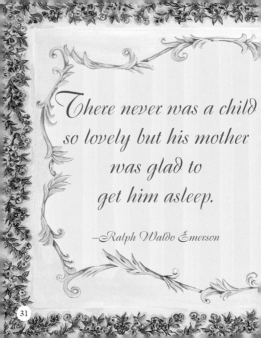

There never was a child
so lovely but his mother
was glad to
get him asleep.

–Ralph Waldo Emerson

Butterfly

Moon

Tulip

Dog

The

mother's

heart is

the child's

schoolroom.

—Henry Ward Beecher

Six Weeks Old

He is so small,

he does not know

35

the summer sun, the winter snow;
  The spring that ebbs and comes again,
All this is far beyond his ken.
  A little world he feels and sees:
His mother's arms, his mother's knees;
  He hides his face against her breast,
And does not care to learn the rest.

–Christopher Morley

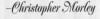

Hickory dickory dock,
The mouse ran up the clock,
The clock struck one,
The mouse ran down;
Hickory dickory dock.

A baby is an angel

whose wings decrease

as his legs increase.

—French Proverb

Pat-a-cake, Pat-a-cake,
baker's man,
Bake me a cake
as fast as you can;
Pat it and prick it,
and mark it with

B,

Put it in the oven
for baby and me.

Off to Slumber Land

Come, winkin', blinkin' sleepyhead,
It's time for you to be in bed
And safe in Slumber Land.
Climb up here on Mother's knee,
My rocking chair our ship will be,
We'll sail across the starlit sea
To far-off Slumber Land.

44

*For all my nieces
and nephews–*
XOXO.

Tracy